BORDEAUX PANORAMA

Yves Simone thanks Cécile Dantarribe.

© Éditions Sud Ouest, 2013
Graphic creation : Camille Bonnier
Ce livre a été imprimé par Legoprint (Italie)
ISBN : 978-2-81770-256-8
N° éditeur : 01.02.03.13

Photographs by Pascal Moulin
Text by Yves Simone

BORDEAUX PANORAMA

Preface by Alain Juppé

English Edition translated by Angela Caldwell

ÉDITIONS SUD OUEST

PREFACE

Is there a different way of showing Bordeaux? A different way of looking at it? Can it be given a new dimension? In *Panoramic Bordeaux*, you'll find our city's most emblematic places shown from such an unusual angle that it sometimes takes a second or two to recognise them, even if you walk past them every day. The unusual views and the momentary surprise when you see the photographs are what give this book its richness and very special depth.

The images are also a striking summary of the urban development that has been ongoing since 1995 to give the city back its attractiveness and modernity, for the people who live here and for the visitors who flock here in increasing numbers every year. As you turn the pages of this book, you'll find it difficult to remember the blackened frontages of the buildings, the motorways cutting through the city centre and the districts that were abandoned for too long. And yet....

Panoramic Bordeaux is already the Bordeaux of the future, for Bordeaux changes every day. There is still some way to go, though. Over the next few years, the Bacalan-Bastide and Jean-Lacques Bosc bridges will be renovated, new housing districts will be built beside the docks, Bastide-Niel will grow up around the St-Jean railway station, the riverside park will be laid out along the right bank, and much more will be done.

This *Panoramic Bordeaux* is the Bordeaux we love.

ALAIN JUPPÉ
Mayor of Bordeaux

INTRODUCTION

In the beginning was the river, a waterway shaken by the tides from the largest estuary in Europe. The river was the Garonne forming a broad sweeping curve between the hillside of Lormont and Floirac, its waters swollen by the rivers Peugue and Devèze, creating a natural harbour that would be known as Port de la Lune.

For many years, historians dated the founding of Bordeaux to the 3rd century B.C. when a Celtic tribe, the Bituriges Vivisci, settled here among the people of Aquitaine. Lately, though, during restoration work on the Grand Hôtel de Bordeaux opposite the Grand Theatre, archaeologists showed that, in the 6th century B.C., there was already a settlement here consisting of timber houses covering an area of six or seven hectares.

Using the original town as its basis, the Romans built the first real town of Bordeaux and named it, *Burdigala*. The origins and meaning of this name are still open to controversy but it led to the modern name of "Bordeaux".
Between the 1st and 2nd centuries A.D. the first Roman settlement was an open town covering 130 to 150 hectares and it already had thoroughfares laid out along east-west and south-north lines. Nowadays, these directions are still recognisable, for example in Cours de l'Intendance, Cours du Chapeau-Rouge and Rue Sainte-Catherine.

In the late 3rd century A.D. the building of robust walls enclosed more than 31 hectares of town, leaving an inner harbour at the mouth of the Devèze. The walls, whose foundations made use of stones from the original Roman settlement, were the subject of great pride for the poet Ausonius.

Although it was the Romans who brought vines to the region, the first major period for the wines of Bordeaux from a commercial point of view was the Middle Ages. The recent marriage of Eleanor of Aquitaine and Henry II Plantagenet, King of England, was to change the town's fortunes. Bordeaux sold its wine; England, in return, sold its wool and salt fish etc. The one person who best symbolised this alliance was Richard II who was born on the banks of the Garonne. He was better-known as the Black Prince and he was immortalised by Shakespeare. Because he was christened here, in St. Andrew's Cathedral, he was also called "Richard of Bordeaux". Much of Northern Europe bought wine from Bordeaux and the surrounding area (up to 100,000 barrels). The town prospered. A second wall was built in the 13th century, shortly followed by a third in the 14th century and the town now stretched over an area of 70 hectares, encompassing the districts of Sainte-Eulalie, Saint-Michel, Sainte-Croix and the new convents in the northern suburbs. This was Bordeaux' first golden age in economic, political and diplomatic terms. In 1453, the French entered the town. Bordeaux, an independent borough that was almost the capital of an independent State, lost much of its glory.

As soon as the town was taken by the French, numerous long-lasting revolts in the 16th and 17th centuries led to the building of three fortresses in the town – Fort Louis in the south (on Place André-Meunier), Fort du Hâ in the west (now the law courts) and Château Trompette in the north (on Place des Quinconces). From then on, Bordeaux was an integral part of the kingdom of France and, as such, it shared the country's fate. With the Renaissance came printing works in the town and the opening of the Collège de Guyenne which had, among its pupils, the Humanist Michel de Montaigne.

The district known as Les Chartrons, which was popular with foreigners from Northern Europe, was dotted with wine cellars and warehouses in which to store the barrels of wine.

In the 18th century, Bordeaux was the world's second largest port after London and its prosperity was the stuff of legends. By obtaining a monopoly in trade with the Caribbean islands, the port became a major centre of the triangular trade.

In the 21st century, the city is beginning to come to terms with this period in its history, the time of the slave trade when black Africans were sold by African kings and Arab merchants to white sugar planters in the Caribbean. The erection of the bust of Toussaint Louverture, the installation of memorial plaques and the organisation of special events are all acknowledgements of the pain inflicted on these people.

Sugar from Santo Domingo and numerous spices were sold throughout Europe, bringing immense wealth to the town. King Louis XV sent some of his greatest intendants to Bordeaux – men like Boucher or Tourny. By methodically undertaking urban development, they modernised the mediaeval town and created a fine example of urban Classicism.

It was Intendant Boucher who, despite the reticence of the local people, demolished the old town walls along the river, creating a square on the banks. He supported the king's architect, Jacques Gabriel, in his plan to give Bordeaux a royal square like Place des Victoires in Paris. Gabriel completed the Hôtel des Fermes (tax office) in 1738 and the stock exchange was finished by his son, Jacques Ange Gabriel, in 1749. Place Royale provided the setting for a huge equestrian statue of Louis XV, which disappeared during the French Revolution.

Intendant de Tourny continued the work that had been started by drawing up a coherent plan for the extension of Bordeaux. The moat along the town walls would be filled in, trees would be planted and the surroundings of the town that were once so evil-smelling would become straight avenues and, very quickly, popular places for a stroll. He commissioned the laying out of avenues (called "Cours") to encircle a town dotted with squares and they are still popular with the people of Bordeaux to this day. On the quaysides, Tourny had the mediaeval wall demolished and replaced by a grandiose project – a uniform row of frontages stretching over more than a kilometre. To the north of the bend in the river, the façade of the Chartrons is part of this urban expansion, with new buildings which, unlike the earlier ones, are all different to each other.

To link these two parts of the town and skirt Château Trompette, Tourny commissioned a public park that he also wanted to turn into a place for a walk and a place in which merchants could meet and do business. The same people also frequented the Grand Theatre designed by Victor Louis, considered in its day to be one of the most beautiful theatres in Europe.

At the same time, many parliamentarians and merchants had luxurious private mansions built throughout the town.

The French Revolution and, more especially, the days of the Napoleonic Empire and the Continental Blockade put a sudden stop to this prosperity. Not until the Restoration of the Monarchy did the ruined town slowly begin to wake up again thanks to colonial trade, wine, high-sea fisheries and trade with the West Indies redirected towards Latin America etc. The economic revival led to the renaissance of the urban planning projects that had been abandoned since the Revolution. Inaugurated in 1822, the Stone Bridge with its seventeen arches marked the beginning of Bordeaux' expansion along the right bank. In addition to the demolition of Fort Louis, Fort du Hâ and Fort du Vieux Marché, Château Trompette was also reduced to rubble, a plan first mooted during the reign of Louis XVI. This left space for the building of a grandiose urban district around Place des Quinconces, the largest square in Western Europe! Opening onto the river, it was designed like a Roman circus ending in a semicircle on the town side. In 1828, the rostral columns overlooking the Garonne were topped with statues of Mercury and Navigation in a style reminiscent of Ancient Rome. With their anchors, caducei and ships' bows, they highlight the importance of the harbour for Bordeaux.

This was also a time of clearances, "realignments" and, if necessary, concealments to give the frontages of the buildings greater effect. A large part of mediaeval Bordeaux disappeared, much to Victor Hugo's regret. On the other hand, Bordeaux' monumental 18th-century improvements were completed and extended by the work of architects and town councillors who looked back nostalgically at Bordeaux' golden era.

Major new projects were also launched in the second half of the 19th century including the hospital (*hôpital Saint-André*), the law courts, university faculties, museums, markets, the first railway station (*gare d'Orléans*) and, shortly afterwards, a second station (*gare du Midi*).

Despite a constantly increasing population (from 90,000 in 1801 and 123,000 in 1851 to 252,000 in 1891), Bordeaux lost its demographic pre-eminence over France's other major cities. Yet it enjoyed an industrial boom thanks, among other things, to shipbuilding, the birth of metalworking and the chemical industry.

After the First World War, concerted action on the part of the town council led to an intense period of building. On 1 August 1929, the town adopted plans for numerous significant amenities, most of them built of concrete. They included the warehouses on the quaysides, the town's gas supply, the sports stadium, the swimming pool in Rue Judaïque and the labour exchange. Yet although the buildings are new and innovative, their architecture still bear traces of reasoned Classicism. This is, after all, Bordeaux!

As to private houses in Bordeaux, they followed the fashion for Art Déco architecture in the area around the sports stadium and the many housing developments along the boulevards although the vitality of the neo-18th century style has remained in evidence. In the 1960s, as in many other towns in France, large housing developments joined the urban landscape. New bridges were built and Le Lac district was created while the old Mériadeck district was demolished to leave way for a compact four-hectare complex of multi-storey buildings. Local people find it difficult to believe that this district could be appreciated by fans of 1970s architecture, and yet it is.

The creation of a 150-hectare conservation area led to an initial phase of embellishment and restoration for the architecture in Bordeaux dating from its golden age. The work is continuing, with the ongoing resurfacing and repointing of the buildings on the quaysides and the re-appropriation of the river banks for pedestrians. This has been accompanied by the creation of gardens and the building of the "mirror" on the quays. The introduction of the tram redesigned the urban landscape, giving local people and visitors alike a new opportunity to enjoy what connoisseurs were already describing as "the most beautiful river frontage in Europe".

All these efforts were eventually recognised and rewarded when the town of Bordeaux was added to Unesco's World Heritage list. Even better, the listing covers more than half the area of the town of Bordeaux, a total of 1,800 hectares, making this the largest urban area to receive recognition from the organisation. The historic old town with its unrivalled 18th-century architecture, the boulevards, the Grand Parc development, the Mériadeck district and the suburbs of Bordeaux combine ancient and modern for a single, noble, beautiful cause.

THE STONE BRIDGE

The idea of building a bridge over the Garonne was considered on several occasions by the enlightened minds of the 18th century. Napoleon, frustrated by the time it took for his Grand Army to pass through the town on its way to Spain, ordered its building in 1810 but, in fact, it was Bordeaux' rich merchants who financed the construction until 1822, by which time France had regained its monarchy. With its 17 arches and a length of 487 metres, the *Pont de Pierre* is a technical feat achieved by engineer Claude Deschamps. Its pillars had to withstand the violence of the river and the power of the tides. From then on, the river and maritime harbours were separated and Bordeaux was linked to the right bank, which was soon to become part and parcel of the town.

PLACE DE
LA BOURSE

Place Royale, which was created in the 1730s, created an opening in the walls encircling a town that had, until then, turned its back on the river. With this square, the Gabriels, architects from Versailles, introduced the French Classical style to Bordeaux with Mansart-style slate roofs and, of course, the masks that would soon be seen all over the town. In those days, the square resembled a balcony overlooking the river. The Garonne was much closer than it is today and the quaysides did not yet exist. The car parks of the 1990s have been removed and only the tram runs through the fully renovated square that is still waiting for the boats...

THE MIRROR OF WATER

Laid out over an underground warehouse dating from the 1930s, the *Miroir d'eau* reflects the buildings on Place de la Bourse, adding a touch of poetry, magic and enchantment to the layout of the quays. Every 15 minutes, countless aluminium spouts create an equally large number of geysers, producing an ephemeral "mist". From the splashes of children to the click-clack of adults, few can resist the charms of this contemporary design, which echoes the square that best symbolises Bordeaux' Classicism.

THE GRAND THEATRE

Completed in 1780 after seven years of work, the *Grand Théâtre* designed by Parisian architect Victor Louis is the finest historic building in Bordeaux. Its twelve massive columns rising over a height of two storeys and topped by twelve statues of muses and goddesses, are a reminder of the architecture of the Ancient Greeks and Romans, a style that was very fashionable at that time. In addition to its role in the Arts, the building housed the French parliament, the National Assembly including M.P. Victor Hugo, during the Franco-Prussian War of 1870. Although it remains a temple of classical music and dance in Bordeaux, its peristyle is also a popular meeting-place for teenagers and couples in love as well as an essential landmark for tourists.

THE WAREHOUSES

Built to store merchandise in the interwar years at a time when Bordeaux' harbour still lay within the town, the *hangars* obstructed the view of the town from the river and the view of the river from the town. After the 1960s, however, they served no useful purpose and, since then, some of them have been demolished, creating a panoramic view that was further improved by the addition of the garden on the quaysides. Other have been kept, restored and redeveloped as delightful places to shop or stop for a bite to eat. In fact, the long promenade beside the river has become one of the town's attractions.

PLACE DE LA VICTOIRE

With its triumphal arch, Place de la Victoire, which was commissioned by Intendant Tourny in the middle of the 18th century, still has several houses built in identical style with arcades, square upper storeys and slate roofs with dormer windows. The 19th century broke the symmetry by laying out new streets and building the Faculty of Medicine. The square is still filled with students (these days, of sociology) who remain here until late at night. The pyramidal column is praiseworthy because, for the first time in Bordeaux, it pays homage to wine. Not before time!

COURS DU
CHAPEAU-ROUGE

Sloping gently down towards the river, Cours du Chapeau-Rouge has a row of apartment blocks on the right-hand side built between the 16th and 20th centuries. Opposite is the much more uniform, and splendid, alignment of buildings known as the "Ilot Louis". All the buildings are the same height and topped by an identical balustrade. All have the same decorative features on the *piano nobile*. These buildings were erected from 1770 onwards, taking some twenty years to complete, and were commissioned by the town's richest merchants. Their frontages have now been cleaned and renovated so that the north and south facades have become worthy of the Grand Theatre to which they lead so majestically.

THE PARK

When the *jardin public* was redesigned in the 19th century, it became an educational and didactic spot, as well as being a place for fun. The natural history museum opened its doors and there was a botanic garden, a bandstand, a model farm etc. It also became a place of instruction and edification, with statues of great men and great artists, preferably from Bordeaux. They include the artist Carle Vernet and the creators of Bordeaux' oenology, Ulysse Gaillon and Alexis Millardet. The town also had to pay homage to Rosa Bonheur. Born in Bordeaux, she was one of the most famous people of her day, an animal painter and emancipated woman whose works still hold pride of place in many of the great art galleries in the USA.

THE CAILHAU GATE AND QUAYSIDES

The two mediaeval gates that have survived in Bordeaux are the 13th-century *Grosse Cloche* (bell tower) and the *Porte Cailhau* dating from the 15th century. It is both defensive (it was originally part of the town walls) and a commemorative triumphal arch. It has an murder hole, slit windows and machicolations as well as a number of Renaissance features such as the statue of King Charles VIII and windows topped by accolade arches. An engraving by a 17th-century Dutch artist shows boats tied up at the foot of the Cailhau Gate. This just shows how far the Garonne has receded! Since the 18th century the gate has been part of the southern frontage on the quays, one of Europe's most grandiose sets of architecture from the Age of Enlightenment. All the buildings are the same height and have the same slate roof, the same architectural style, the same decorative features etc. In fact, it is a uniquely well-ordered façade!

THE BOTANIC GARDEN

A new district was built on former industrial wasteland in La Bastide, with housing, offices, a university and a botanic garden. This long strip of land provided an opportunity to create vistas of the new district and undertake some innovative development. The garden is divided into six "worlds" illustrating the main natural environments in Gironde, from the limestone cliffs on the right bank of the river to the sand dunes of the Atlantic coast. The innovative garden breaks with the traditions of conventional botanic gardens since ecology, sustainable development and learning are its main driving forces.

PLACE DES QUINCONCES

The Girondins' memorial stands proudly in the centre of the semicircular Place des Quinconces which, as people like to remind you, is the largest square in Western Europe. The existence of such an impressive square in the town centre today is explained by the erstwhile existence of a Vauban fortress here, marking the north of Bordeaux. The square was laid out between 1815 and 1825. In 1830, the rostral columns were erected, opening up a superb view from the esplanade down over the river. The columns are topped by a statue of Navigation and one of Mercury symbolising trade. In 1858, two huge statues were added to the square, paying homage to philosophers Montaigne and Montesquieu, both of whom came from Bordeaux. On the top of his column, a winged demi-god holds broken chains in his right hand, symbolising the Liberty that the Republic wanted to spread throughout the world.

THE GIRONDINS MEMORIAL

The monument des Girondins is still waiting... for its Girondins. The statues of the local members of parliament were never made so they never took their places on the memorial. Never mind! Since work ended in 1902, the locals have always referred to the quadriga and their extraordinary allegories of Republic and Concord as "the Girondins' horses". Some of these animals, taken straight from a fantasy tale, have webbed feet and fish tails; others have claws and dragons' tails. They symbolise the Republic or Concord crossing the oceans to carry the ideals of the all-conquering Third Republic to lands far away. The Republic is accompanied by allegories of Justice, Police, mandatory Schooling etc. The horses disappeared during the German Occupation but were reinstated by Mayor and Resistance fighter, Jacques Chaban-Delmas. They have been restored by the current town council.

PLACE DU PARLEMENT

Place du Parlement, formerly Place du Marché-Royal, connected Place de la Bourse to the town centre from 1750 onwards. Although completed in the 19th century, the buildings all have the same three storeys – an arcaded ground floor and two square upper floors distinctly separated by string-courses. Overall, the buildings are decorated with masks and brackets and topped by a balustrade. This was the first square in old Bordeaux to be renovated in the 1980s and it attracted numerous restaurants, giving it the ambiance of a Mediterranean town as soon as the first rays of the sun hit it, a far cry from its reputation as a cold, middle class English city. Around it are the hustle and bustle of the Saint-Pierre district.

THE ARCADE

The *Galerie bordelaise* was built between 1830 and 1837, funded by the fortune of a grandson of the Viceroy of Mexico. Its external austerity contrasts with the mercantile luxury on the inside – marble columns with gilded capitals, mirrored pilasters, superb lighting etc. This "shopping arcade" cuts diagonally through a group of buildings and it took advantage of the latest developments of its time such as metal-framed construction, gas lighting, fire protection etc. Although it is now awaiting restoration worthy of its beauty and its history, the *Galerie bordelaise* remains one of the outstanding success stories of neo-Classical architectural design.

THE GALLIEN PALACE

Built in the early 3rd century A.D., the *Palais Gallien* was the town's amphitheatre, the scene of gladiatorial combat and other traditional entertainments in the days of the Ancient Romans. It gets its name from a mediaeval legend claiming that Charlemagne built the palace for his wife, Gallienna. Although in ruins, the layout of the elliptical building was visible in its entirety until the French Revolution when it was sold off as a national asset and quickly demolished. Entire portions of the building were integrated into houses round about and all that remains of the palace today are its entrance and a few arches, the only surviving reminder of the Ancient Roman settlement of *Burdigala*.

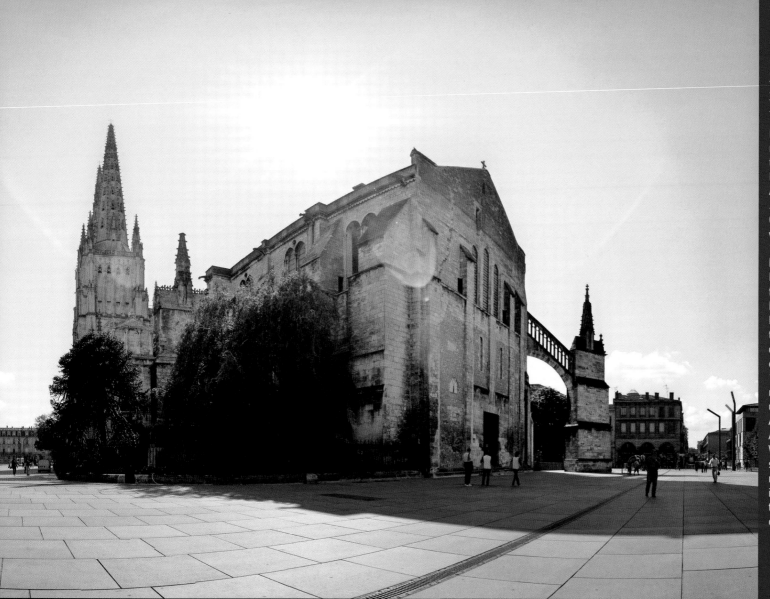

PLACE PEY-BERLAND

Place Pey-Berland has been returned to pedestrians, enabling them to see and appreciate two of Bordeaux' historic buildings, St. Andrew's Cathedral (*cathédrale Saint-André*) in the Romanesque, Gothic and Renaissance styles with part of it completed in the 19th century, and the Town Hall (*Hôtel de Ville*) built before the French Revolution as a palace for Archbishop Ferdinand-Maximilien Mériadeck de Rohan. Deprived of its West Front, the cathedral concentrates its decorative features on the 14th-century north door. However, the 13th-century royal entrance is a reminder that the cathedral was used for the weddings of Eleanor of Aquitaine and Louis VII and, later, Anne of Austria and Louis XIII. With its ceremonial portico separating the street from the main courtyard, the Rohan Palace is, with the Grand Theatre, one of the two most significant late 18th-century buildings in Bordeaux.

ST. ANDREW'S CATHEDRAL

The wide nave, which still has rounded Romanesque arching on the north side, is now roofed with quadripartite ribbed vaulting with liernes and tiercerons from various periods in its history. They have been restored several times. The majestically massive nave extends into a slender chancel that is striking for its consistency. Its undeniable elegance comes from the perfection of its ethereal architectural lines dating back to a period between the end of the 13th and middle of the 14th centuries.

THE LAW COURTS

Only two stone towers remain of Fort du Hâ and they are now an integral part of the court complex that includes the 19th-century law courts, the magistrates' college built in the 1970s and seven contemporary wooden towers containing the seven courtrooms that make up the *Tribunal de Grande Instance*. Behind their glass enclosure and emerging from their undulating copper roof, the wooden shells seem to be levitating on concrete cupolas that overlook the bustle of the street below. They are designed to give an image of a more serene, more transparent form of justice. This building is one of the success stories as regards contemporary architecture in Bordeaux.

PLACE CAMILLE JULLIAN

The name Camille Jullian is that of a specialist in Roman history who wrote the first "History of Bordeaux from its Origins to 1895", a work based on the scientific and archaeological methods of the 19th century. The monument on this square is dedicated to him. It consists of stones from the Ancient Roman Burdigala that were uncovered in the town.

St. Simeon's Church has had an eventful history. After the French Revolution, the building in the shape of a ship's hull was used as a naval college. A local man then turned it into a cannery and, in 1874, patented an easy-opening system for sardine cans. Yes indeed, it was a man from Bordeaux who invented the key used to open tins of sardines! The building then became a garage until, in the 2000s, it was turned into an art house cinema, the *Utopia*, that is bringing new visitors to the square.

CONTENTS